Renee

# The Moon

## By Carmen Bredeson

**Consultants**
Orsola De Marco, Ph.D.
Department of Astrophysics
American Museum of Natural History
New York, New York

Jeanne Clidas, Ph.D.
National Literacy Consultant

Katy Kane
Educational Consultant

SCHOLASTIC INC.
New York  Toronto  London  Auckland  Sydney
Mexico City  New Delhi  Hong Kong  Buenos Aires

Designer: Herman Adler Design
Photo Researcher: Caroline Anderson
The photo on the cover shows the Moon.

No part of this publication may be reproduced in whole or in part,
or stored in a retrieval system, or transmitted in any form or by any means,
electronic, mechanical, photocopying, recording, or otherwise,
without written permission of the publisher. For information regarding permission,
write to Permissions Department, Grolier Incorporated, a subsidiary of
Scholastic Inc., 90 Old Sherman Turnpike, Danbury, CT 06816.

ISBN 0-516-24491-4

Copyright © 2003 by Children's Press, a division of Scholastic Inc. All rights reserved.
Published by Scholastic Inc., 557 Broadway, New York, NY 10012.
A ROOKIE READ-ABOUT® is a trademark and/or registered trademark of
GROLIER PUBLISHING CO., INC. SCHOLASTIC and associated logos are trademarks
and/or registered trademarks of Scholastic Inc.

12 11 10 9 8 7 6 5 4                    4 5 6 7 8 9/0

Printed in the U.S.A.                          61

First Scholastic paperback printing, February 2004

What are those dark areas
that make the moon look
like a face?

A volcano on Earth

They are pools of hard lava. Long ago, hot lava gushed out of volcanoes on the Moon. It cooled and became hard.

From Earth, the dark lava looks like the "Man in the Moon."

The Moon was probably once a part of Earth.

A huge rock from space hit Earth four billion years ago. It blasted off chunks that became the Moon.

8

The Moon has many
big holes called craters
(CRAY-turs).

Space rocks make craters
when they crash into
the Moon.

Most of the craters are
very old.

The Moon is about one-fourth the size of Earth.

Imagine cutting Earth into four pieces. The Moon would be the size of one of those pieces.

12

The Moon does not have any light of its own. It reflects light from the Sun like a mirror reflects light.

The Moon goes all the way around Earth every four weeks.

During its trip, different parts of the Moon reflect sunlight toward Earth.

16

That is why the Moon
seems to change shape.

The amount of the Moon
that we see changes.

Sometimes the Sun shines on the whole side of the Moon that faces Earth. Then we see a full moon.

19

Sometimes we see only
a quarter of the Moon.

Other times we see just a
tiny sliver, called a crescent
(KRESS-uhnt).

Sometimes we see no
moon at all.

We saw the Moon up
close for the first time
in 1969. That is when
astronauts landed there.
We saw the landing
on television.

The astronauts had to wear big space suits and tanks of air. There is no air to breathe on the Moon.

Twelve astronauts have
walked on the Moon.
They brought 800 pounds
of Moon rocks home
to Earth.

Scientists study the rocks
to learn about the Moon.

27

Would you like to touch
a Moon rock? You can
touch one at museums
in Texas, Florida, and
Washington, D.C.

Imagine sliding your
fingers across a real
piece of the Moon!

# Words You Know

astronaut

crater

crescent

full moon

space suit

volcano

# Index

# About the Author

Carmen Bredeson has written dozens of nonfiction books for children. She lives in Texas and enjoys traveling and doing research for her books.

# Photo Credits

Photographs © 2003: Corbis Images: 20 (Michael & Patricia Fogden), 3 (Bob Krist), 12, 27, 30 bottom (Roger Ressmeyer); NASA: cover, 24, 31 top right; NASA/Jet Propulsion Lab Photo: 11; National Air and Space Museum: 28; Photo Researchers, NY: 4, 31 bottom (E.R. Degginger), 23, 30 top left (NASA), 19, 31 top left (David Nunuk/SPL), 15 (John Sanford/SPL), 16 (Eckhard Slawik/SPL), 7 (Joe Tucciarone/SPL); Photri Inc./NASA: 8, 30 top right.